WASHINGTON REDSKINS

BY BARRY WILNER

The Child's World

Published by The Child's World®
1980 Lookout Drive • Mankato, MN 56003-1705
800-599-READ • www.childsworld.com

Acknowledgments
The Child's World®: Mary Berendes, Publishing Director
Red Line Editorial: Editorial direction
The Design Lab: Design
Amnet: Production

Design Element: Dean Bertoncelj/Shutterstock Images
Photographs ©: G. Newman Lowrance/AP Images, cover;
Tom Rothenberg/ZumaPress/Icon Sportswire, 5; Paul
Spinelli/AP Images, 7; Rusty Kennedy/AP Images, 9; Ray
Carlin/Icon Sportswire, 11; Anders Brownworth/Shutterstock
Images, 13; Pablo Martinez Monsivais/AP Images, 14–15; Tom
DiPace/AP Images, 17; J. Scott Applewhite/AP Images, 19;
David Stluka/AP Images, 21; Pro Football Hall of Fame/AP
Images, 23; Richard Lipski/AP Images, 25; Jeff Haynes/AP
Images, 27; Al Messerschmidt Archive/AP Images, 29

ISBN 9781634070065
LCCN 2014959711

Printed in the United States of America
Mankato, MN
July, 2015
PA02265

ABOUT THE AUTHOR

Barry Wilner has written 41 books, including many for young readers. He is a sports writer for The Associated Press and has covered such events as the Super Bowl, Olympics, and World Cup. He lives in Garnerville, New York.

TABLE OF CONTENTS

GO, REDSKINS!

T he Washington Redskins started as the Boston Braves in 1932. They were renamed the Redskins the next year. The team moved to Washington, D. C., in 1937. It is the capital of the United States. The Redskins have had some great success there. Washington has awesome fans. They have stuck by their team through ups and downs. Let's meet the Redskins.

Running back Alfred Morris (46) fights for yardage during a game against the Jacksonville Jaguars on September 14, 2014.

WHO ARE THE REDSKINS?

The Washington Redskins play in the National Football **League** (NFL). They are one of the 32 teams in the NFL. The NFL includes the American Football Conference (AFC) and the National Football Conference (NFC). The winner of the NFC plays the winner of the AFC in the **Super Bowl**. The Redskins play in the East Division of the NFC. Washington has won three Super Bowls. The Redskins also won two NFL Championship Games before the Super Bowl began after the 1966 season.

Quarterback Mark Rypien passed for 292 yards and two touchdowns in Washington's Super Bowl win on January 26, 1992.

WHERE THEY CAME FROM

Owner George Preston Marshall did not think Boston's fans cared enough about his football team. Marshall even moved the NFL Championship Game from Boston to New York in 1936. He then moved the Redskins to Washington, D.C., in 1937. They won the NFL Championship that year. Washington did not make the playoffs from 1946 to 1970. But coach George Allen turned the team around. He led the Redskins to the playoffs five times from 1971 to 1976. Joe Gibbs took over in 1981. He won three Super Bowls with Washington from 1982 to 1991.

In 1972, coach George Allen led the Redskins to their first Super Bowl.

WHO THEY PLAY

The Washington Redskins play 16 games each season. With so few games, each one is important. Every year, the Redskins play two games against each of the other three teams in their division. Those teams are the New York Giants, Philadelphia Eagles, and Dallas Cowboys. The Cowboys are Washington's biggest **rival**. The two teams have played each other more than 100 times. The Redskins love trying to take down the Cowboys.

The Redskins and Cowboys have played each other at least once each year since 1960.

WHERE THEY PLAY

The Redskins have played in three home stadiums. Their first home in Washington, D.C., was Griffith Stadium. They shared it with the Washington Senators baseball team. The Redskins moved to D.C. Stadium in 1961. It was renamed RFK Stadium in 1968. In 1997, Jack Kent Cooke Stadium opened in Landover, Maryland. It holds 85,000 fans. It is one of the largest stadiums in the NFL. The stadium was renamed FedEx Field in 1999.

Every season, FedEx Field draws more fans than most other NFL stadiums.

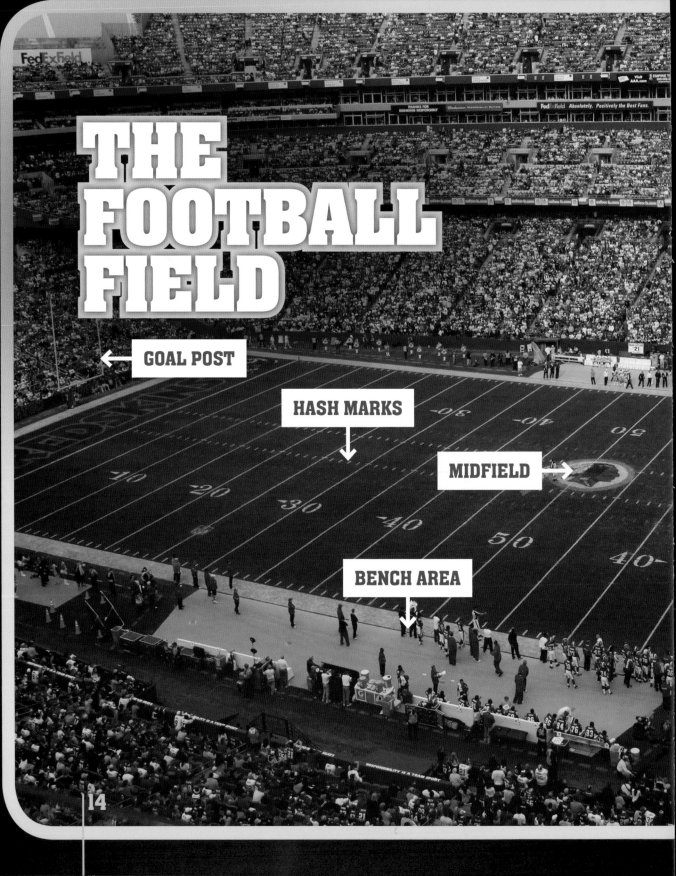

THE FOOTBALL FIELD

GOAL POST

HASH MARKS

MIDFIELD

BENCH AREA

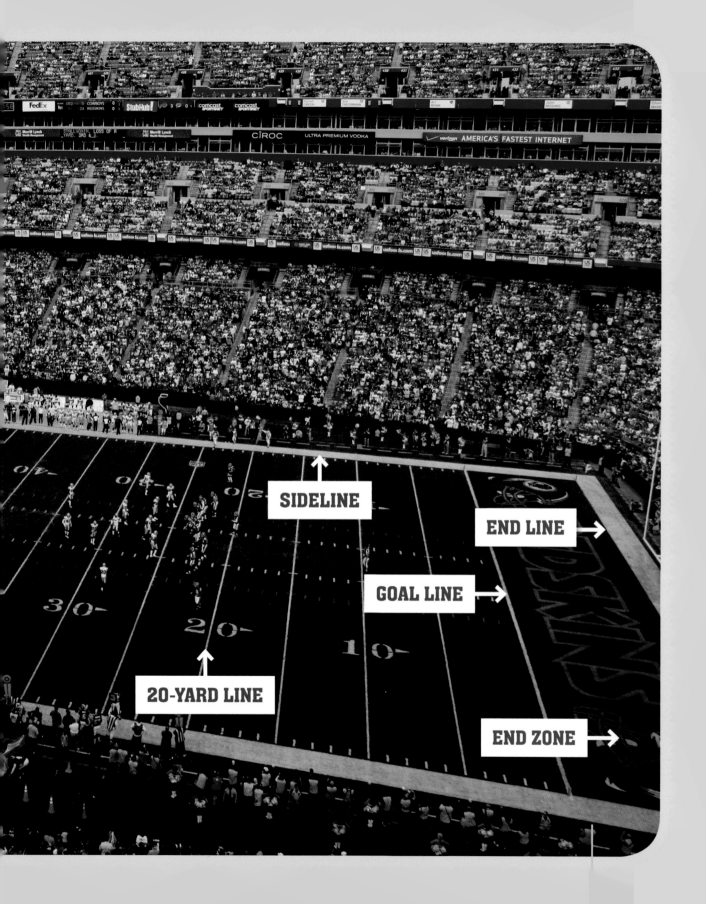

BIG DAYS

The Redskins have had some great moments in their history. Here are three of the greatest:

1937—The Redskins' first year in Washington, D.C., was special. Quarterback Sammy Baugh led the team. Washington went 8-3 and played the Chicago Bears in the NFL Championship Game. Baugh passed for 352 yards in a 28-21 victory.

1981—Joe Gibbs was hired as head coach on January 13. He had been a successful offensive **coordinator**. He had never been a head coach. But he became one of the best. He led the team from 1981 to 1992 and 2004 to 2007.

Coach Joe Gibbs is carried off the field after Washington beat the Buffalo Bills 37-24 in the Super Bowl on January 26, 1992.

1987—The Redskins won their second Super Bowl in six years. They beat the Denver Broncos 42-10 on January 31, 1988. Doug Williams became the first black quarterback to win the big game. He threw four **touchdown** passes in the second quarter.

TOUGH DAYS

Football is a hard game. Even the best teams have rough games and seasons. Here are some of the toughest times in Redskins history:

1940—Washington played one of the worst games ever. On December 8, the Redskins lost the NFL Championship Game 73-0 to the Chicago Bears. The fact it was a home game made it even worse.

1985—The Redskins played the New York Giants on November 18. Quarterback Joe Theismann was tackled in the second quarter. His leg got stuck underneath him and broke. Other players could hear the crack. Theismann never played again.

Quarterback Joe Theismann lies on the ground after breaking his leg against the New York Giants on November 18, 1985.

2012—Another Washington quarterback got **injured**. Star **rookie** Robert Griffin III hurt his knee on December 9. The injury got worse in the playoffs. He had to have surgery after the season. He and the team struggled the following year.

MEET THE FANS

The Redskins had a famous group of fans that wore pig costumes. They did it to honor the big guys on the offensive line. The linemen were known as "The Hogs." So the fans called themselves "The Hogettes." Some of them even wore funny dresses to games. "Hail to the Redskins" is the team's fight song. It was first played at a game in 1938.

"The Hogettes" were some of the most unique fans in the NFL.

HEROES THEN

Sammy Baugh spent all of his 16 seasons with the Redskins. He led the NFL in passing yards four times. He also led the league in passing touchdowns twice. Baugh made six **Pro Bowls**. John Riggins played for Washington from 1976 to 1985. He was not very fast for a running back. But he was powerful. Riggins shined in big games. He is the leading rusher in team history. Defensive back Darrell Green played 20 NFL seasons for the Redskins. He was one of the fastest players in the NFL. The team trusted him to cover great receivers by himself.

Sammy Baugh played quarterback, tailback, punter, and defensive back for the Redskins during his 16-year career.

HEROES NOW

Robert Griffin III was the Offensive Rookie of the Year in 2012. He is a threat to run or throw on every play. Injuries have slowed him down. But he is one of the most exciting players in the league when he is healthy. Running back Alfred Morris also started playing in 2012. He finished second in the NFL in rushing yards that season. Wide receiver Pierre Garcon has strong hands. He uses his speed to get open. He led the league with 113 catches in 2013.

Quarterback Robert Griffin III is one of the most exciting players in the NFL when healthy.

GEARING UP

NFL players wear team uniforms. They wear helmets and pads to keep them safe. Cleats help them make quick moves and run fast. Some players wear extra gear for protection.

THE FOOTBALL

NFL footballs are made of leather. Under the leather is a lining that fills with air to give the ball its shape. The leather has bumps or "pebbles." These help players grip the ball. Laces help players control their throws. Footballs are also called "pigskins" because some of the first balls were made from pig bladders. Today they are made of leather from cows.

Speedy wide receiver DeSean Jackson joined the Redskins in 2014.

HELMET

SHOULDER PADS

GLOVES

THIGH PADS

FOOTBALL

CLEATS

SPORTS STATS

Here are some of the all-time career records for the Washington Redskins. All the stats are through the 2014 season.

PASSING YARDS

Joe Theismann 25,206

Sonny Jurgensen 22,585

TOTAL TOUCHDOWNS

Charley Taylor 90

John Riggins 85

RECEPTIONS

Art Monk 888

Charley Taylor 649

INTERCEPTIONS

Darrell Green 54

Brig Owens 36

SACKS

Dexter Manley 91

Charles Mann 82

POINTS

Mark Moseley 1,206

Chip Lohmiller 787

Redskins running back John Riggins led the NFL in rushing touchdowns in 1983 and 1984.

RUSHING YARDS

John Riggins 7,472

Clinton Portis 6,824

GLOSSARY

coordinator an assistant coach who is in charge of the offense or defense

injured when a player gets hurt

league an organization of sports teams that compete against each other

Pro Bowl the NFL's All-Star game where the best players in the league compete

rival a team whose games bring out the greatest emotion between the players and the fans on both sides

rookie a player playing in his first season

Super Bowl the championship game of the NFL, played between the winners of the AFC and the NFC

touchdown a play in which the ball is held in the other team's end zone, resulting in six points

FIND OUT MORE

IN THE LIBRARY

Frisch, Aaron. *Super Bowl Champions: Washington Redskins*. Mankato, MN: Creative Books, 2014.

Snider, Rick and Charley Casserly. *100 Things Redskins Fans Should Know & Do Before They Die*. Chicago, IL: Triumph Books, 2014.

Temple, Ramey. *Inside The NFL: Washington Redskins*. New York: Av2, 2014.

ON THE WEB

Visit our Web site for links about the Washington Redskins:
childsworld.com/links

Note to Parents, Teachers, and Librarians: We routinely verify our Web links to make sure they are safe and active sites. So encourage your readers to check them out!

INDEX